# YOU'RE
# NOT OLD
# YOU'RE
# VINTAGE

summersdale

YOU'RE NOT OLD, YOU'RE VINTAGE

Research by Sarah Viner

Summersdale Publishers Ltd
46 West Street
Chichester
West Sussex
PO19 1RP
UK

www.summersdale.com

Printed and bound in the Czech Republic

ISBN: 978-1-84953-533-5

Substantial discounts on bulk quantities of Summersdale books are available to corporations, professional associations and other organisations. For details contact Nicky Douglas by telephone: +44 (0) 1243 756902, fax: +44 (0) 1243 786300 or email: nicky@summersdale.com.

TO.............................................

FROM..........................................

YOU DON'T GET OLDER,
YOU GET BETTER.

Shirley Bassey

WITH MIRTH AND
LAUGHTER LET OLD
WRINKLES COME.

William Shakespeare

EVENTUALLY YOU WILL
REACH A POINT WHEN
YOU STOP LYING ABOUT
YOUR AGE AND START
BRAGGING ABOUT IT.

Will Rogers

YOU CAN'T TURN BACK
THE CLOCK. BUT YOU CAN
WIND IT UP AGAIN.

Bonnie Prudden

PEOPLE SAY I'M INTO
MY SECOND CHILDHOOD.
THE REALITY IS THAT
I NEVER LEFT MY
FIRST ONE.

Spike Milligan

# GROW OLD ALONG WITH ME! THE BEST IS YET TO BE.

Robert Browning

# THE GOOD OLD
# DAYS ARE NOW.

Tom Clancy

THE THREE AGES OF
MAN: YOUTH, MIDDLE
AGE, AND 'MY WORD YOU
DO LOOK WELL'.

June Whitfield

NICE TO BE HERE?
AT MY AGE IT'S NICE
TO BE ANYWHERE.

George Burns

I WILL NEVER GIVE
IN TO OLD AGE UNTIL
I BECOME OLD. AND I'M
NOT OLD YET!

Tina Turner

A DIPLOMAT IS A
MAN WHO ALWAYS
REMEMBERS A
WOMAN'S BIRTHDAY
BUT NEVER
REMEMBERS HER AGE.

Robert Frost

AGE IS AN ISSUE OF
MIND OVER MATTER.
IF YOU DON'T MIND,
IT DOESN'T MATTER.

Mark Twain

IF WRINKLES MUST
BE WRITTEN UPON OUR
BROWS, LET THEM NOT
BE WRITTEN UPON
THE HEART.

James A. Garfield

YOU CAN LIVE TO
BE 100 IF YOU GIVE
UP ALL THE THINGS
THAT MAKE YOU WANT
TO LIVE TO BE 100.

Woody Allen

WHEN IT COMES TO
OLD AGE WE'RE ALL
IN THE SAME BOAT,
ONLY SOME OF US HAVE
BEEN ABOARD A
LITTLE LONGER.

Leo Probst

AN ARCHAEOLOGIST IS
THE BEST HUSBAND A
WOMAN CAN HAVE. THE
OLDER SHE GETS THE
MORE INTERESTED HE
IS IN HER.

Agatha Christie

I WANT TO LIVE TO BE
120. THAT'S WHEN I
WILL START WORRYING
ABOUT MY AGE.

Helena Christensen

# THE BEST TUNES
# ARE PLAYED ON THE
# OLDEST FIDDLES.

Ralph Waldo Emerson

WHENEVER THE TALK
TURNS TO AGE, I SAY
I AM 49 PLUS VAT.

Lionel Blair

ONE SHOULD NEVER
TRUST A WOMAN WHO
TELLS HER REAL AGE.
IF SHE TELLS THAT,
SHE'LL TELL ANYTHING.

Oscar Wilde

THE FIRST SIGN OF
MATURITY IS THE
DISCOVERY THAT THE
VOLUME KNOB ALSO
TURNS TO THE LEFT.

Jerry M. Wright

# GROWING OLD IS COMPULSORY, GROWING UP IS OPTIONAL.

Bob Monkhouse

IT'S IMPORTANT TO
HAVE A TWINKLE IN
YOUR WRINKLE.

Anonymous

I DON'T WANT TO RETIRE.
I'M NOT THAT GOOD AT
CROSSWORD PUZZLES.

Norman Mailer

# WE ARE ALWAYS THE SAME AGE INSIDE.

Gertrude Stein

THE SECRET TO
STAYING YOUNG IS TO
LIVE HONESTLY, EAT
SLOWLY AND LIE
ABOUT YOUR AGE.

Lucille Ball

ONE OF THE GOOD
THINGS ABOUT
GETTING OLDER IS
YOU FIND YOU'RE MORE
INTERESTING THAN
MOST OF THE PEOPLE
YOU MEET.

Lee Marvin

I LOVE EVERYTHING
THAT'S OLD: OLD
FRIENDS, OLD TIMES,
OLD MANNERS, OLD
BOOKS, OLD WINE.

Oliver Goldsmith

# YOUTH HAS NO AGE.

Pablo Picasso

TO ME, OLD AGE
IS ALWAYS 15 YEARS
OLDER THAN I AM.

Bernard Baruch

OLD AGE IS LIKE
EVERYTHING ELSE.
TO MAKE A SUCCESS OF
IT, YOU'VE GOT TO
START YOUNG.

Theodore Roosevelt

# A MAN GROWING OLD
# BECOMES A CHILD AGAIN.

Sophocles

I DON'T FEEL OLD.
I DON'T FEEL ANYTHING
TILL NOON. THAT'S WHEN
IT'S TIME FOR MY NAP.

Bob Hope

I USED TO THINK
I'D LIKE LESS GREY
HAIR. NOW I'D LIKE
MORE OF IT.

Richie Benaud

# THE MAN OF WISDOM IS
# THE MAN OF YEARS.

Edward Young

# YOUTH DISSERVES;
# MIDDLE AGE CONSERVES;
# OLD AGE PRESERVES.

Martin H. Fischer

AT MY AGE 'GETTING
LUCKY' MEANS FINDING
MY CAR IN THE
PARKING LOT.

Anonymous

I'LL KEEP
SWIVELLING
MY HIPS UNTIL
THEY NEED
REPLACING.

Tom Jones

AS YOU GET OLDER, THE
PICKINGS GET SLIMMER,
BUT THE PEOPLE DON'T.

Carrie Fisher

THE EASIEST WAY
TO DIMINISH THE
APPEARANCE OF
WRINKLES IS TO KEEP
YOUR GLASSES OFF
WHEN YOU LOOK IN
THE MIRROR.

Joan Rivers

ONE OF THE BEST
PARTS OF GROWING
OLDER? YOU CAN
FLIRT ALL YOU LIKE
SINCE YOU'VE BECOME
HARMLESS.

Liz Smith

BEING 80 MAKES
ME FEEL LIKE AN
AUTHORITY, ESPECIALLY
WHEN I SAY,
'I DON'T KNOW.'

Peter Ustinov

JUST REMEMBER,
WHEN YOU'RE OVER THE
HILL, YOU BEGIN TO
PICK UP SPEED.

Charles M. Schulz

OLD MEN ARE FOND OF GIVING GOOD ADVICE, TO CONSOLE THEMSELVES FOR BEING NO LONGER IN A POSITION TO GIVE BAD EXAMPLES.

François de La Rochefoucauld

I'M NOT SURE THAT OLD
AGE ISN'T THE BEST
PART OF LIFE.

C. S. Lewis

THE WHITER MY HAIR
BECOMES, THE MORE
READY PEOPLE ARE TO
BELIEVE WHAT I SAY.

Bertrand Russell

AS WE GROW OLDER,
OUR BODIES GET
SHORTER AND OUR
ANECDOTES LONGER.

Robert Quillen

IF YOU RESOLVE TO GIVE
UP SMOKING, DRINKING
AND LOVING, YOU DON'T
ACTUALLY LIVE LONGER;
IT JUST SEEMS LONGER.

Clement Freud

WHEN GRACE IS JOINED
WITH WRINKLES, IT IS
ADORABLE. THERE IS AN
UNSPEAKABLE DAWN IN
HAPPY OLD AGE.

Victor Hugo

I ABSOLUTELY REFUSE
TO REVEAL MY AGE.
WHAT AM I – A CAR?

Cyndi Lauper

# A PRUNE IS AN EXPERIENCED PLUM.

John H. Trattner

SOME PEOPLE REACH
THE AGE OF 60
BEFORE OTHERS.

Lord Hood

# YOU'RE ONLY YOUNG ONCE, BUT YOU CAN ALWAYS BE IMMATURE.

Dave Barry

BIRTHDAYS ARE GOOD
FOR YOU. STATISTICS
SHOW THAT THE PEOPLE
WHO HAVE THE MOST
LIVE THE LONGEST.

Larry Lorenzoni

# THERE'S ONE ADVANTAGE TO BEING 102. THERE'S NO PEER PRESSURE.

Dennis Wolfberg

AGE MERELY SHOWS
WHAT CHILDREN
WE REMAIN.

Johann Wolfgang von Goethe

TIME AND TROUBLE WILL
TAME AN ADVANCED
YOUNG WOMAN, BUT AN
ADVANCED OLD WOMAN
IS UNCONTROLLABLE BY
ANY EARTHLY FORCE.

Dorothy L. Sayers

THE AGEING PROCESS
HAS YOU FIRMLY IN ITS
GRASP IF YOU NEVER
GET THE URGE TO
THROW A SNOWBALL.

Doug Larson

SEIZE THE MOMENT.
REMEMBER ALL
THOSE WOMEN ON
THE *TITANIC* WHO WAVED
OFF THE DESSERT CART.

Erma Bombeck

I'M AIMING BY THE TIME I'M 50 TO STOP BEING AN ADOLESCENT.

Wendy Cope

I DON'T KNOW HOW
I GOT OVER THE HILL
WITHOUT GETTING
TO THE TOP.

Will Rogers

AGE ISN'T HOW OLD
YOU ARE BUT HOW
OLD YOU FEEL.

Gabriel García Márquez

A BIRTHDAY IS JUST THE
FIRST DAY OF ANOTHER
365-DAY JOURNEY
AROUND THE SUN.
ENJOY THE TRIP.

Anonymous

WE DON'T STOP PLAYING
BECAUSE WE GROW OLD;
WE GROW OLD BECAUSE
WE STOP PLAYING.

George Bernard Shaw

IF I HAD MY LIFE TO
LIVE OVER AGAIN,
I'D MAKE THE SAME
MISTAKES, ONLY SOONER.

Tallulah Bankhead

WHEN I WAS A
BOY THE DEAD SEA
WAS ONLY SICK.

George Burns

CHERISH ALL YOUR
HAPPY MOMENTS; THEY
MAKE A FINE CUSHION
FOR OLD AGE.

Christopher Morley

YOUTH IS THE TIME FOR
ADVENTURES OF THE
BODY, BUT AGE FOR THE
TRIUMPHS OF THE MIND.

Logan Pearsall Smith

ALLOW ME TO PUT
THE RECORD STRAIGHT.
I AM 96 AND HAVE BEEN
FOR SOME YEARS PAST.

Erica Jong

# EVERYONE IS THE AGE
# OF THEIR HEART.

Guatemalan proverb

EVERYTHING SLOWS
DOWN WITH AGE, EXCEPT
THE TIME IT TAKES
CAKE AND ICE CREAM
TO REACH YOUR HIPS.

John Wagner

# I INTEND TO LIVE FOREVER, OR DIE TRYING.

Groucho Marx

EACH YEAR IT GROWS
HARDER TO MAKE ENDS
MEET — THE ENDS I
REFER TO ARE HANDS
AND FEET.

Richard Armour

MY GRANDMOTHER IS OVER 80 AND STILL DOESN'T NEED GLASSES. DRINKS RIGHT OUT OF THE BOTTLE.

Henny Youngman

ANOTHER BELIEF OF
MINE: THAT EVERYONE
ELSE MY AGE IS AN
ADULT, WHEREAS I AM
MERELY IN DISGUISE.

Margaret Atwood

I'M HAPPY TO
REPORT THAT MY
INNER CHILD
IS STILL
AGELESS.

James Broughton

AGE DOES NOT
DIMINISH THE EXTREME
DISAPPOINTMENT OF
HAVING A SCOOP OF
ICE CREAM FALL
FROM THE CONE.

Jim Fiebig

WHITE HAIR OFTEN
COVERS THE HEAD, BUT
THE HEART THAT HOLDS
IT IS EVER YOUNG.

Honoré de Balzac

I DON'T BELIEVE
IN AGEING. I BELIEVE
IN FOREVER ALTERING
ONE'S ASPECT TO
THE SUN.

Virginia Woolf

AGE SELDOM ARRIVES
SMOOTHLY OR QUICKLY.
IT'S MORE OFTEN A
SUCCESSION OF JERKS.

Jean Rhys

# THE BEST
# MIRROR IS
# AN OLD FRIEND.

George Herbert

AGE IS JUST A
NUMBER. IT'S TOTALLY
IRRELEVANT UNLESS, OF
COURSE, YOU HAPPEN TO
BE A BOTTLE OF WINE.

Joan Collins

YOU'RE GETTING OLD
WHEN THE ONLY THING
YOU WANT FOR YOUR
BIRTHDAY IS NOT TO BE
REMINDED OF IT.

Anonymous

THE OLDER WE GET, THE
BETTER WE USED TO BE.

John McEnroe

MY HUSBAND'S IDEA OF
A GOOD NIGHT OUT IS A
GOOD NIGHT IN.

Maureen Lipman

IF I COULD GET BACK MY
YOUTH I'D DO ANYTHING
IN THE WORLD, EXCEPT
GET UP EARLY, TAKE
EXERCISE OR BE
RESPECTABLE.

Oscar Wilde

I BELIEVE IN LOYALTY.
WHEN A WOMAN
REACHES A CERTAIN
AGE SHE LIKES, SHE
SHOULD STICK WITH IT.

Eva Gabor

OLD AGE AND TREACHERY
WILL ALWAYS BEAT
YOUTH AND EXUBERANCE.

David Mamet

THE KEY TO SUCCESSFUL
AGEING IS TO PAY AS
LITTLE ATTENTION TO
IT AS POSSIBLE.

Judith Regan

# YOUTHFULNESS IS ABOUT HOW YOU LIVE NOT WHEN YOU WERE BORN.

Karl Lagerfeld

# I'M TOO OLD TO DO THINGS BY HALF.

Lou Reed

FUN IS LIKE LIFE
INSURANCE; THE OLDER
YOU GET, THE MORE
IT COSTS.

Kin Hubbard

I CAN STILL ENJOY
SEX AT 74. I LIVE AT 75,
SO IT'S NO DISTANCE.

Bob Monkhouse

IN YOUTH WE RUN
INTO DIFFICULTIES. IN
OLD AGE DIFFICULTIES
RUN INTO US.

Beverly Sills

# TO STOP AGEING —
# KEEP ON RAGING.

Michael Forbes

WE TURN NOT OLDER
WITH YEARS, BUT NEWER
EVERY DAY.

Emily Dickinson

# ALL WOULD LIVE LONG, BUT NONE WOULD BE OLD.

Benjamin Franklin

# AGE IS ONLY
# A NUMBER.

Lexi Starling

ANYONE WHO KEEPS THE
ABILITY TO SEE BEAUTY
NEVER GROWS OLD.

Franz Kafka

OLD AGE IS AN
EXCELLENT TIME FOR
OUTRAGE. MY GOAL IS
TO SAY OR DO AT LEAST
ONE OUTRAGEOUS THING
EVERY WEEK.

Maggie Kuhn

I MUST BE GETTING OLD.
I CAN'T TAKE YES FOR
AN ANSWER.

Fred Allen

WHEN IT COMES
TO STAYING YOUNG,
A MINDLIFT BEATS A
FACELIFT ANY DAY.

Marty Bucella

IF YOU WANT A THING
WELL DONE, GET A
COUPLE OF OLD BROADS
TO DO IT.

Bette Davis

GROWING OLD IS NO
MORE THAN A BAD HABIT
WHICH A BUSY MAN HAS
NO TIME TO FORM.

André Maurois

AS YOU GET OLDER
THREE THINGS HAPPEN.
THE FIRST IS YOUR
MEMORY GOES... AND I
CAN'T REMEMBER THE
OTHER TWO.

Norman Wisdom

AUTUMN IS THE
MELLOWER SEASON,
AND WHAT WE LOSE
IN FLOWERS, WE MORE
THAN GAIN IN FRUITS.

Samuel Butler

IT TAKES A LONG TIME
TO BECOME YOUNG.

Pablo Picasso

OLD AGE ISN'T SO
BAD WHEN YOU
CONSIDER THE
ALTERNATIVE.

Maurice Chevalier

# IF YOU REST, YOU RUST.

Helen Hayes

YOU CAN JUDGE YOUR
AGE BY THE AMOUNT OF
PAIN YOU FEEL WHEN
YOU COME IN CONTACT
WITH A NEW IDEA.

Pearl S. Buck

# LAUGHTER DOESN'T REQUIRE TEETH.

Bill Newton

MEN ARE LIKE WINE —
SOME TURN TO VINEGAR,
BUT THE BEST IMPROVE
WITH AGE.

C. E. M. Joad

# GROWING OLD IS NOT GROWING UP.

Douglas Horton

LIVE YOUR LIFE AND
FORGET YOUR AGE.

Norman Vincent Peale

OLD AGE IS LIKE A
PLANE FLYING THROUGH
A STORM. ONCE YOU
ARE ABOARD THERE IS
NOTHING YOU CAN DO.

Golda Meir

SOME DAY YOU WILL
BE OLD ENOUGH TO
START READING FAIRY
TALES AGAIN.

C. S. Lewis

THE OLDER ONE GROWS,
THE MORE ONE LIKES
INDECENCY.

Virginia Woolf

ALAS, AFTER A
CERTAIN AGE EVERY
MAN IS RESPONSIBLE
FOR HIS FACE.

Albert Camus

I DON'T PLAN TO GROW
OLD GRACEFULLY. I PLAN
TO HAVE FACELIFTS
UNTIL MY EARS MEET.

Rita Rudner

YOU KNOW YOU'RE
GETTING OLD WHEN THE
CANDLES COST MORE
THAN THE CAKE.

Bob Hope

OLDER PEOPLE
SHOULDN'T EAT HEALTH
FOOD, THEY NEED ALL
THE PRESERVATIVES
THEY CAN GET.

Robert Orben

# I'M 60 YEARS OF AGE. THAT'S 16 CELSIUS!

George Carlin

YOU CAN'T HELP
GETTING OLDER, BUT
YOU DON'T HAVE
TO GET OLD.

George Burns

YOUTH IS THE GIFT OF
NATURE, BUT AGE IS A
WORK OF ART.

Garson Kanin

EVEN IF THERE'S
SNOW ON THE ROOF,
IT DOESN'T MEAN THE
FIRE HAS GONE OUT IN
THE FURNACE.

Anonymous

I'M LIKE OLD WINE. THEY
DON'T BRING ME OUT
VERY OFTEN, BUT I'M
WELL PRESERVED.

Rose Kennedy

I DON'T NEED YOU TO
REMIND ME OF MY AGE.
I HAVE A BLADDER TO DO
THAT FOR ME.

Stephen Fry

MEN CHASE GOLF
BALLS WHEN THEY'RE
TOO OLD TO CHASE
ANYTHING ELSE.

Groucho Marx

# THE OLDER I GET, THE OLDER OLD IS.

Tom Baker

FORTY IS THE OLD AGE
OF YOUTH; 50 THE
YOUTH OF OLD AGE.

Victor Hugo

# YOU ONLY LIVE ONCE, BUT IF YOU DO IT RIGHT, ONCE IS ENOUGH.

Mae West

INSIDE EVERY OLD
PERSON IS A YOUNG
PERSON WONDERING
WHAT HAPPENED.

Anonymous

NOBODY LOVES LIFE
LIKE HIM THAT'S
GROWING OLD.

Sophocles

# THE LONGER I LIVE THE MORE BEAUTIFUL LIFE BECOMES.

Frank Lloyd Wright

WISDOM DOESN'T
NECESSARILY COME
WITH AGE. SOMETIMES
AGE JUST SHOWS UP
ALL BY ITSELF.

Tom Wilson

# THE YOUNG SOW WILD OATS. THE OLD GROW SAGE.

Winston Churchill

DO NOT WORRY ABOUT
AVOIDING TEMPTATION.
AS YOU GROW OLDER IT
WILL AVOID YOU.

Joey Adams

THE OLD BELIEVE
EVERYTHING, THE
MIDDLE-AGED SUSPECT
EVERYTHING,
THE YOUNG KNOW
EVERYTHING.

Oscar Wilde

I'M LIKE A GOOD CHEESE.
I'M JUST GETTING
MOULDY ENOUGH TO
BE INTERESTING.

Paul Newman

I ADVISE YOU TO
GO ON LIVING SOLELY
TO ENRAGE THOSE
WHO ARE PAYING YOUR
ANNUITIES. IT IS THE
ONLY PLEASURE I
HAVE LEFT.

Voltaire

# YOUTH IS A WONDERFUL THING. WHAT A CRIME TO WASTE IT ON CHILDREN.

George Bernard Shaw

I REFUSE TO ADMIT I'M
MORE THAN 52, EVEN
IF THAT DOES MAKE MY
SONS ILLEGITIMATE.

Nancy Astor

# I RECENTLY TURNED 60. PRACTICALLY A THIRD OF MY LIFE IS OVER.

Woody Allen

LAUGH LIKE YOU'RE 10,
PARTY LIKE YOU'RE 20,
TRAVEL LIKE YOU'RE 30,
THINK LIKE YOU'RE 40,
ADVISE LIKE YOU'RE 50,
CARE LIKE YOU'RE 60,
LOVE LIKE YOU'RE 70.

Anonymous

# DON'T LET AGEING GET YOU DOWN. IT'S TOO HARD TO GET BACK UP.

John Wagner

I'M AT AN AGE WHEN
MY BACK GOES OUT
MORE THAN I DO.

Phyllis Diller

# LOOKING 50 IS GREAT — IF YOU'RE 60.

Joan Rivers

FOR ALL THE ADVANCES IN MEDICINE, THERE IS STILL NO CURE FOR THE COMMON BIRTHDAY.

John Glenn

WRINKLES SHOULD
MERELY INDICATE
WHERE THE SMILES
HAVE BEEN.

Mark Twain

# YOUTH WOULD BE AN IDEAL STATE IF IT CAME A LITTLE LATER IN LIFE.

Herbert Henry Asquith

# TIME IS A DRESSMAKER SPECIALISING IN ALTERATIONS.

Faith Baldwin

OLD AGE: THE CROWN
OF LIFE, OUR PLAY'S
LAST ACT.

Cicero

# I STILL HAVE A FULL DECK; I JUST SHUFFLE SLOWER NOW.

Anonymous

# OLD AGE IS NO PLACE
# FOR SISSIES.

Bette Davis

NO MAN IS EVER
OLD ENOUGH TO
KNOW BETTER.

Holbrook Jackson

# THE GOLDEN AGE IS BEFORE US, NOT BEHIND US.

William Shakespeare

@EsmeTheBird

If you're interested in finding out more about our books, find us on Facebook at **Summersdale Publishers** and follow us on Twitter at **@Summersdale**.

# www.summersdale.com